my light. my best friend. my love.
-our secret-

-z.k.d

MUSE

Poetry&Prose

By: Zachry K. Douglas

you can write all you want.

you can even try to be a poet.

but when the pain hits you,

we all suffer the same.

not everyone understands your power and how long
you've had to walk on fire to get to where you're at.
i see you. i hear you. i am here to love on you and
give you kisses when you least expect them. i was
not only made to spend forever caring for you,
i was made to meet you, my best friend, when
my world was finally able to hold the moon it
had been missing.

separated souls have an easy way of finding each other after the storms pass. there is a particular sound the heart makes when the other is missing.

it goes unnoticed by many, because we all have one created for our twin flame. silence the mind, watch for the signs, and trust the calling. we are not meant to be alone forever with our hands only holding air.

take your time to digest each moment. we have gone through life too long without the other, and i am aching for all of your chaos to make love to mine.
i know we are here because of each other's
presence.

-i can still taste the stars you wore last time-until we breathe in the soul of the other, we will never understand love. a breath can only die if it is being held hostage. time is measured in inches, and i need to be closer to you in order to feel each second i have been without you.

love never gave me a poem until i met you.
within these very tired bones, your strength
keeps holding me up to talk to the moon.
when before, i had already surrendered my
energy to the lines which felt like twenty-five
to life. your heart is filled with beauty and it
spills onto me as if you are painting the
warmest of colors. promise me you'll never
leave, sweet one.

-i will always be in need of the wild you possess-

the language we speak has more
to do with our dreams than it
does with our reality.

not everyone understands that
concept, and fewer will ever
attempt to, but what i have
with you, effort is all i can give.

if i am anything,

i am too much of

something humans

don't want, and a

lot of what humans

cannot understand.

wear something red and tell me you love me.
i'll show you how hands were meant to be
used and how lips can create art by simply
tracing patterns across your shoulder blades.
turning you over, my hands make a direct
path down the front of your body, creating
sparks for the burn we are after. once all
words have been exhausted, curl into me
and place your worries on my chest. i want
to take it all from you so nothing is left but
for you to rest your sweet soul next to mine.
inhaling the moonlight, our hearts become
the luminescent beginning to every orphaned
dream before us.

being able to hand over all of the secrets you've kept
hidden in the pockets of your soul for years without
breathing a single word of them, allows your lungs
the opportunity to grow with your body for once,
instead of being the reason why you never could
grow with the universe. consuming all of the
sweetness that is now entangled in my bones,
i have never been more full off of another human
in my entire life. they now rise with gratitude and
fall with peace.

she's lived her whole life under the gun with
her parents and society. the only time she
smiles is when she's nervous. it's terribly
awkward being alive in a world where so
many are barely breathing and asking
what is wrong when you're out of breath.
she walks where the ocean meets the stars
beneath the dark of night. there's something
about the moon that brings out the truth
when you are desperately seeking some
semblance of self-worth.

please do not give up when love doesn't reach you.
keep fighting for the opportunity to one day be
that for someone. i believe in you and know
humans pretty well. we value reflections of
ourselves in others. a friend is someone
who stays and reflects the soul of your
heart. be that and you will live forever,
because inside of us, is the key that
unlocks hope for the hopeless.

i know who you are down to the very strands of hair laying on my chest. i will always want to be a part of the complete circle my arms make when they find your waist in the middle of the night. not everyone gets to see beautiful the way i see it. that's how i know you are the love inside my heart.

i am in the middle of what i call my own life.
it's hard to understand at times, but i know
for certain it is finally moving forward;
forward with you. forward with us.
a movement that had always escaped
me, grabbed me by the soul and led me
to your love. something i can say i never
felt worthy of until you told me,
"just breathe, i got you."

she knew she could, so she did. a woman like her can do
more than just move mountains. she becomes them and
anything else people have told her she never would be.
within her moment of freedom, she found a lifetime
of wild to love. her destiny is now in the hands of her
own for the first time, and the grip will not relinquish
what was always meant to be for this ineffable creature.
she's jupiter living in the flesh; tolerant and expansive.
her mind is a weapon that has been known to take
back the night. she's a dandelion in a field of
wildflowers, continuously competing against
herself to make those around her feel as if they
aren't just weeds others had told them they were.

i adore the way the stars hum in her darkness. her bones are made of river stones and smells of freshly picked sunsets. her religion is anything that makes her soul flutter, which tends to call out in the middle of the night for the ache of everything life has to offer.

it's okay to be your own muse and love yourself in a

world teaching you that you need someone to do it for

you. don't be incapable of providing your own shelter.

fear gives birth to the little voice inside
of your head telling you whatever comes
next has the likelihood of breaking you.

don't shut the door. break the motherfucker
down and welcome it. you must remember
how precious this life is and how fragile we
all really are.

a breath cannot be substituted nor can it forget
the willingness you have for a dream only you
can see.

before you take your heart out,
make sure your hands can hold
the stars. be as soft as you can
with a love you have gone your
whole life without.

    precious things are not grown
    under pressure, and love is
    no different.

my mind is full of handpicked
emotions, and as it grows, i grow
with it. strange things happen once
you figure out that living under the
sun, not all of the light goes where
you need it. it goes where it wants to,
because it has to in order to reach
whatever aches inside of you.

i want you any way i can get you. not because you are
gorgeous and sexy. not because you are witty and kind.
not because you are independent and strong. there is
no one else like you, and i will never wish to start a
single second of my life without seeing you in it.
my good days are a product of your love.

to all the wild dancing around
us, may we be lost forever.

may we remain a furious fire for
anything out there which touches
our souls and ignites a dance we
carry inside.

you showed me how beautifully human it is to give someone something they could never give back and still smile and love as if i just promised you a lifetime of adventures, knowing how empty my pockets were. we are here now, and i will be living my life in honor of that moment you gave me to make sure we are full on every step we take towards the next jump in front of us. and if for some reason we should fall, may we be able to give it every goddamn ounce of soul it takes to make it back up and try again. it's who we are. we have never been good at giving up, because the pain taught us how daring it is to be unforgettable.

we all want someone who can understand that
we won't always have good days and still be
there to hold us after we fall apart. love is
knowing we all hurt and break differently.
it's not always written out or spoken,
but pain still has a voice.

i will go through all the misery if it means being able to look over at you while we are sleeping and knowing we are both safe and together in the same bed, under the same stars, breathing in the same dreams, and knowing we will still be fucking crazy for each other when our bodies finally surrender our souls.

being human means feeling
lost while completely in love
with things others find strange
and meaningless. there is no
middle ground when you are
searching for yourself.

throughout life, you will continue to heal. it's the kind of process that you'll fold in and out of your soul with as the years fade from your eyes. but you must be patient and kind to every emotion, feeling, and heart-scream you encounter. they are all lessons, and from them, you will embrace the softness of how the moon feels against your skin while you fall asleep on her breasts. it's a maddening part of being human, but once you find your sweet spot, the fruit will always fall for you.

i am always trying to find more of myself. whether it be in humans, pictures, books, music, heartache, or a random smile, i am searching. my curse is i cannot rest, and within it, i am constantly aware i may never discover anything more than struggle.

she asked me, "how do you fall asleep like you do?"

closing the distance between us,

i whispered in her ear,

"by counting your breaths as you lie next to me."

i am in love with the way you sleep. you never disturb the universe. you are soft as rain and fall into me like the lightest snowflake ever made. i love how my body reacts when i wake up and yours is next to mine.
eyes like yours weren't made to be closed for long, because sweet adventures await an awakened dreamer like you.

i love the way you look when you get out of the shower and sit in front of the mirror. i can see myself stepping out with you and us playing like little kids before we get ready to head out the door. i cannot wait to get home and be there again with you and soak in everything we are. i look forward to things like that. even though it is a few hundred miles down the road from where we are now, i can still see what we are fighting for and what the ultimate goal is for us.

i love how your soul breathes and wanders off with the night sky. how you chase after everything you love until your wings need rest. and after you have caught your breath, your feet always keep running towards a life and love you will never settle for.

we create our world and i want every idea and
thought you have to be involved in its creation.

without it, i don't work the same. i stop meaning
a goddamn thing without you.

i held her as tight as i could, and asked her,
"how do you feel?"

she gently smiled, and said to me,
"i love that you ask me that."

i responded in truth and matching her eyes,
"i care about you all the time. i want to know
if your energy is good. if you are feeling well.
if you are tired. if you are feeling anything
that i need to help with or love on more.
i always will."

she is the blanket i need when i feel alone and lonely.
the kind that makes you warm, comfortable, and able
to sleep through a night you pretended to be wasn't
there, just so you could close your eyes and imagine
a life and time where the pain was gone and
everything felt fucking whole. my shivers then,
are my goosebumps now when she holds me.

i have caught glimpses of your brilliance before when
you didn't know i was watching. your laugh bounces
off the sky and lands softly in my chest. your smile
gives life to everything around it and it repays you
by loving the parts you have kept under your skin
for reasons only known to you. your eyes tell me
chapters others don't have the soul to read and i
cannot seem to put you down at any point during
my day. your heart has this immense beauty about
it, as if it is holding all the moons around us.
your hands have a tendency to wander in waters
unbeknownst to other seagoing life. your lungs
have the capacity to be filled with the unattainable
and you breathe without regret. you love to love
and i love you based on that fact alone.
there's nothing in my life more meaningful
than your body showcasing grace and a natural
explanation of why i have starved myself all of
these years just to have my lips on yours. you do
this thing with your legs as i inch towards you,
and right before i am between them, you let me
know i will have to work for what i am after.
but it's all worth it, because you have given me
more than oceans could fill by simply holding
me when i am not strong enough to hold you.
balance is the backbone of time, and she is what
keeps me standing.

we will always have the 2am talks about galaxies,
the universe, and sex. it's what keeps the heart
young. it's what keeps the connection from ever
being broken. it's what keeps the sun up,
hoping it can speak moonish things once
again to the humans below looking for
light and love.

kiss the flowers and tell them your troubles. humans tend to have problems understanding each other. it's why there will always be bouquets bought for the endless visits to where we buried more than a body.

i make sure to hold your hand before i close my eyes.
i do that because i don't feel safe enough to encounter
my own dreams by myself. i do not feel safe without
you being close to me. maybe that is a fatal flaw,
but it is a flaw i am willing to live with if it means
you never know how it feels.

i carry you within my bones at all times. each step i take, we make together. there is nothing greater in this world than knowing your existence is a reason why someone smiles at you with the force of all the stars behind it.

before she died, she told me,

    "do not look to the moon to see me.
    do not look to the wind to hear me
    call your name. do not look to the
    oceans to feel me around you.
    only look into your heart,
    for i am going home now."

and with the final breath she drew,
my heart gradually grew in size;
filling all the emptiness that was
left behind by my soulmate saying
goodbye.

a heart that once only kept me alive,
now is forever holding her love inside.
my life is yours and i will live for you.
a life that now beats for two.

i have been thinking about you for a while now and we need to talk. i know and understand there is still love woven into the words in which i speak that may scare you off. but every time i pick up the phone, i press end, hoping i hit the button soon enough. i am afraid there is no longer love hidden in yours. if i never get the courage to finally see the call through, just know i love you and want a life with you, and only you. my soul and i need you to be whole again. so if i call, please pick up, it is important.

i like to watch the stars as the day draws to an end.
not because i am looking for ones that are falling,
but more or less thinking you are looking down at
me, watching over us, as we go through another day
without you. maybe you talk amongst the others and
wish on us humans. maybe you envy us as much as
we envy the brilliance of you all.

i can only imagine what it is like to have your love. how our souls would runaway together and never return. far from this world's reality is where we would create our own. where you and i would go fishing for stars and swim through black holes of eternity. being lost in love with you is what i need.

last night i remembered how your hands would write on my flesh. you would inscribe your confessions and darkest secrets on it. i loved you for that; trusting my soul with your desires and nightmares, hoping they wouldn't bleed into me. not only did those words seep into me, your soul found solace in the arms of mine, as if they wanted to hold each other's pain.

i kissed the moon goodnight
and she felt it from a world
away. a love like ours, stays
with us long after the day
is gone. long after the rain
has fallen. long after the
final kiss of a lifetime.
it goes with the cosmos,
and as it goes, we venture
along with it, making sure
whatever we have can be
found again by our spirits.

love can be a lonely place.
try and not get lost along
the way. too many have
succumbed to this,
and i can only hope
the remaining breaths
you take, never know
the pain a living death
can amass once you
give up your heart for
something that will not
be there to wake you up
in the morning.

all it took was her kiss to melt all of my stars;

creating the moon in my life. the one that

will always guide me home in the middle

of my sleepless nights.

as i place my right hand on the
left side of my chest, i can still
feel your lovely heartbeat.

during my lonely nights,
when the world gets too
loud, i count them to
fall asleep.

i do not need all the extravagant words to impress you.
i just want to love you for the rest of my life. even after
my final goodbye comes in the form of my last breath,
i will wait for you endlessly; until our souls are
reunited again.

i write for someone i have yet to meet, yet she already
knows everything about me. i see myself waking up
next to her for the rest of my life, and i cannot wait
to fall asleep tonight. this time, i know my muse
will be next to me, waiting for moments to turn
into memories. it is finally our turn to just be
happy and not worry about what never was.
from now on, it will forever be, just us.

i want to hold you like no one else has before.
those who have tried, always failed to keep
you safe and whole. their minds will never
fully comprehend how the universe holds
the stars at night;

    softly, peacefully, and lovingly.

being held is a substantial part of understanding
a human. somehow, we always let go too soon or
too late. though at times, we are fortunate enough
to have everything fall into place. if you look to the
sky at night, the most perfect display of devotion
greets those who dare to know the true meaning;
star by star.

living in a moment with you,
is better than living a lifetime
alone. my emptiness tends to
greet me when i am away from
you. though you have told me
before i am never alone, it is
difficult for me to believe that
whenever you leave and take
away the best part about me.

with an anxious look on her face,
she said, "i have shared my entire
life story with you. i bet you think
i am crazy or weird don't you?"

as our souls locked hands, the only
thing i needed to say was, "no dear.
i find you to be human. believe me
when i tell you that's a beautiful
thing. all i ask of you is this:
never stop being yourself around
me. to lose you, i would miss out
on life itself."

our life was far from perfect, but we loved one another for the precious moments when we became each other's shoulder. those times will always be a framed memory which hangs on the walls of my soul. when i am in the struggle, when i think life is getting too heavy to hold, i shall close my eyes, take a deep breath, and realize just how far we have come.

just to see you smile again, my love, i'll give you the one you gave to me. the one that cured all of my aches and pains. the one that covers my face to this day. a smile like that will never allow fear to overtake me, nor will it destroy the essence of my beliefs. i believe in us and the power of giving back to those who have given everything to me.

she has a taste for chaos and her appetite for life is something i often dream about. she is fearless when it comes to the difficult moments this universe continues to confront her soul with. each day, she leaves me licking my lips which are forever coated in her magic; a reminder to me how she will always be the angel who gave me my wings. she saved a shattered spirit and taught it not only how to fly, but how to land without ever touching the ground.

you came into my life when all i needed was a smile
from someone who cared enough to stay with me.
it saved my soul from the depths i had taken it.
now i am able to see another sunrise because of the
moment we made by interlocking our fears with the
idea of forever. all it takes is a glimmer of hope to
transform a tragedy into a beautiful life.

your heart is a song i once composed.
my hands remain in motion, as if
they are leading some type of life in
my direction. as if they know how
to hold what is now gone. a human
who leaves, never takes away everything.
they leave us with just enough to know
we will always carry a part of them with
us wherever we go. my arms are still
trying to comprehend the concept of
love being a limb of your own and
going on without knowing the function
of not holding what is now gone.

i regret not having made memories with
you yet. it is as simple as that when it
comes to how i feel about what we could
become. of what we might be one day.
of all the things i have only wished for
with you. one day, time will allow us to
be with each other for more than just a
few hours every couple of years.

    and when that day arrives, i will be on one
    knee, asking you to never leave me again.

every night the stars mourn and cry
out. for they have lost one of their
own. it was the night you fell from
the universe's grasp. it was an
intoxicating ride to see you fall
and land next to me. now all the
stars use their powers to assimilate
their shine in your eyes.

in the end, it was love that
completely destroyed their
hearts.

it was forgiveness that helped
pick up the pieces.

it was hope that made it beat
again.

it was the soul that empowered
them to find peace in a broken
heart.

after being tormented for years, she used her poem like a nickel plated .45; murdering the devil behind her. now she dances in his ashes, like a young child running through the rain; soaking in all of the pleasures he once took away.

what i would give just to taste you again.
your skin was the sweetest of all forbidden
fruit. then for dessert, i would kiss your
soul so deeply, even they would be
speaking in tongues.

"i will take a dozen of those red roses."

right then, i knew what she was going to say, "you must be in trouble or are you going to surprise her?"

with my face turning a shade of red it seldom sees, i explained to her, "no, mam. i am not in trouble. i buy a dozen red roses every day to leave for her in a vase so she can see just how much the flowers are jealous of her divine beauty."

she laughed, and said, "that's something you don't hear all the time." shaking my head back and forth, i truthfully said, "well, dear, you've never seen her kind of magic before. i've seen it for sixty-five years and the best thing about it is, our love has kept us alive. no water needed. just love"

i could never be in love with
anyone else as long as you are
on this earth. i could never
promise anyone anything,
because all of my promises,
you keep.

i never knew what it took
to love myself until i met
you. i never knew love to
be something that wanted
to stay. love always left me
in the middle of the night,
when my nightmares
woke me.

i am anything i want
to be with you,

and that's all i have
ever wanted with
someone.

that's all i hope anyone
wants when it comes
to love and all the
unknown it presents
at any given time.

and before she knew it,
everything that had ever
broken her, created a life
many will never get to see.
she isn't hiding from fear,
she is what happens when
fear trembles and becomes
another chapter in a story
that will be read out loud
with pride and strength,
from a voice which had
been silenced for too long.

in life, all we want is someone who doesn't make us feel so alone, because love is nothing without showing them why you continue to choose them every chance you get. it's about reassuring them with shelter between your arms and safety in your eyes. we don't get that many chances at making the most of our time here, but i hope you can see the four walls protecting you and the roof above your head. love is about believing in the best of people, and when you have that, you'll have a best friend who knows your worst, but keeps telling you, "this is us, and we will make it, because i have your back and you have mine." it won't always be the warm sunny days, but i promise you, the rain will never be as sweet. and if you are lucky to find someone like i did, who leaves sand in your bed because she'd rather walk the beaches than run around town, marry her.

for so long i existed so others could feel loved and appreciated, but you've given me bravery to love the parts of me others always closed their eyes to. the parts that were littered with clenched fists and surrendering footsteps. the parts no one dared to interact with because of how foreign they were to them. i am grateful for your constant rising and slow breaths. i am thankful for your gracious hands and unwavering closeness. i am myself, because you are my circle, and with that, you are the very soul of my own. you have always been the words attached to my lungs, begging to taste something genuine and exhale the boy who was clinging to safety; afraid of letting go and maturing into the man i never thought i could be.

-you are the bones that allow me to stand tall, sweet one-

poetry is made to messy and misunderstood.
for our brains and thoughts are of our own.
to find humans that understand the words
in which you try and convey, is an explosion
of dying stars that is hard to fathom.
creating and birthing an idea not only you
believe, but others do as well, is a lost form
of communication and feeling these days.
in order to believe in yourself, you must
first believe that your wishes have never
gone unnoticed. you must believe you
are them.

the love that i have lost,
is the kind that will never
leave me.

and that in itself, is a
beautiful tragedy.
it is a mourning which
is buried deep in the sun.
a slow and steady burn
that never dies, but keeps
you moving forward,
hoping you never have
to stare into it for too long.

whenever you feel alone, do not close
your eyes and turn off your soul to the
world. leave your mind wide open so
that your heart will always be able to
experience the light.

remember, if they are against us,
the stars will always be for us.
the night sky is filled with dreamers
like you and i. but if the sky should
fall on us tomorrow, i hope every
single star hits me while i am still
alive.

i would rather experience a life of
believing in my dreams than see
someone else take all of my
sky away from me.

i loved you so much that i wanted to
bring you everything everyone had
ever taken away from you.

to this day, i still express the same
feeling. i am still trying to recover
everything you have had taken
from you. you deserve that effort.
you fucking deserve that kind of
devotion and love. you are the
most precious of all things
living, and i will treat you as
such always without expecting
or wanting anything in return.

some people will never respect you or your story,
but to someone it will be their favorite book.
for i would read every page and look at
every picture if that could mean me
learning more about you.

if the stars do not lead you to me,
i will beg for my soul to shine
bright enough for you to see how
i will always be home when
darkness invades your life.
i will fucking give my life to
see it through.

as the dying wind separated the leaves
from the trees, i knew it was time
to go. all the signs started making sense
to me, as if i had a pocket full of wishing
pennies to hopefully throw back into
the peaceful sea.

before i left, your tears said it all,
our endless love was lost when
summer turned into fall.

a romantic affair between two
rebellious teenagers, thinking
love would save them from
goodbye, ended up without
each other, forever lost in a
place where love danced away
with the passing clouds
in the sky.

every summer, i go back to the old
oak tree that rests above the pond.
for it is where we both threw our
hearts into the water, wishing for
the love between us to never
drown.

she asked me,

> " how do you know we are supposed to be together?"

i answered her softly,

> "my soul will always love you. it will always be an adventure when i smother your body with my love. because we are soulmates. we were chosen to meet at this exact moment of forever. i have been talking to an angel at night."

you make me smile;

as if it has known you before.
as if it has kissed your dreams.
as if it has seen you grow old.
as if it has seen all of the sunsets
we have witnessed together.
as if it knows the same things
about mine.

when i looked at her, i thought to myself,

> "there is nothing more beautiful
> than a naked soul who undresses
> her worries and fears in front of
> you."

even her lonely bones spoke of being afraid to fly;
for they had never taken flight before.

> i told her,

>> "i will always fly beside you."

> she cried out,

>> "thank you for seeing through me for all
>> i am not."

i put my arms around her and closed my eyes,
softly whispering in her ear,

> "together, we will forever be as one.
> where you go, i go."

that night, we soared above the clouds of our past and
quietly landed in each other's grasp; holding on for dear
life. as we made love by candle light, the silhouette of
our souls danced on the ceiling of the universe; making
shadows for the world to see.

in the beginning stages, love was
undefined until two wandering
souls met while collecting stars
in the sky.

on that night, love forever changed.
you see, to a human, it is a word
which gets abused and used in a way
that cheats the very reason their souls
met in the first place. souls define the
word as the sole purpose of life.

they never knew anything but love,
and they cannot stand to see such
a beautiful thing, mean so little
to us humans.

in you, i have found a place where my hands are allowed
to move without knowing the direction. they wander all
day across the canvas of your heart, sketching out
dreams from the night before. in you, i have found a
place where i can be honest about the hurt i still feel
from the pain i inflicted upon myself. in you, i have
found new truth about love and the way it embraces
the broken who swore it off because they could never
fully regain the function of breathing. in you, i have
found places where my lips are able to kiss you deeper
than the drowning waters you had been treading.
help me be good, sweet woman, and teach me your
smile so i can use it when i feel lost. i know if i ever
hurt you, i will be hurting myself, and that's
unacceptable, because i hold you above any other living
thing. in you, i have found that two souls can be forged
by fire and come out speaking with flowered tongues.
if i ever forget why i am still here, i look at her, and she
smiles, because it all lives and dies within her.

during any of the four seasons,
you have a chance of coming
back to me.

and here i wait in winter,
for a summer's beginning.

on our way home today, i saw her staring out of the window. it wasn't an odd thing to see, but i could tell something was on her mind. something someone said or did to her. i reached over to take her hand and placed it in mine. we finally made a red light and i leaned over to kiss her cheek, then whispered into her ear,

"it's the wild that keeps you beautiful."

never give up your pursuit
of everything that makes
you feel alive and loved.

though death never misses,
you still have time to find
what it's afraid of. you still
have time to be free.

i am here to learn, appreciate, and love you.
i am not seeking to control any aspect of
your world. you managed this far without
me and do not need anyone telling you how
to live your life. i just want to know you better
through the art you touch and the words you
hold back when the day attempts to steal away
your smile.

there is an infinite way in

how i love, and i love the

love we have bonded

between us.

if you wait for her,
she will become the
moon that had been
missing from your sky,

the imagination
you were taught
to never use,

and the magic you went
without, but always
believed you could see.

when the moon remembers

who you are, all else is

forgiven. even the scars that

stare back at you become

teary eyed, as the flesh weeps

for your love once again.

when it comes to you and i,
there is no hesitation in my
love for you. there is no
second guessing who i will
fall for each time i see you
open your eyes and close
them to go dream-chasing
with me.

listen softly to the beats.

    they rise
        and fall,
            all for you.

she seems to be always running away from something,
but finds herself each time. she remains grounded in life
until she needs to touch the sky. she's starving for magic
and someone to listen to her and hear her for the first
time. she's aching to be touched and understood.
she will look at you, and i hope you're able to give
her what she's never had or at least try all you can
to make it that way.

even when the day
haunts her, she finds
me and smiles when
she hears me whisper,

"the moon was named after you."

when you grow, i grow.
we are a garden of wild
where love waters the
soul. i am not here to
keep you from the sun.
you are all of the light
in my universe.

my life has never needed
someone else's breath in
order to feel my own lungs,
and here you are,

    still helping me feel human.

look at me and

tell me love is

enough. tell me

you'll stay when

all we have left

are hearts to give.

give me you. give me us. give me a thousand years of
uncertainty and i will show you how to love for today.
i don't know how not to care and i hope that day never
comes. when i think about truth, i realize there are no
regrets when you're chasing sunsets.

there was never an ending
that could take me away
from what we made,
and that's how we still
love. that's how we remain
human despite the possibility
of it not working out in our favor.

all she wants is for you to involve her in
the details of your life. when she shares
those moments with you and they aren't
reciprocated, you will watch her distance
herself more and more until you can no
longer tell her how you feel. she is simply
wanting more of what you've never given,
which can be scary, but what's worse than
that is not being able to share your life
with anyone who will want those parts
after she is gone. don't be the cause of
why it didn't work. care enough to love
her with transparency. anything else kills
the soul and future opportunities to find
someone who will care as much as she did.

one day i am going to meet you and i hope it's not
too late. i hope you are still looking for something
more from this place. i hope you are still trying to
find yourself amongst the fragile moons you keep
clenched in your hands, wishing no one would
ever touch them. i hope you are able to see me
when my soul has been directed towards you
since the first time we met, back when this
world was still being gathered by the stars
before us. i hope you can hear the silence
surrounding who i used to be long enough
to appreciate my articulation for the journey
i presently find myself on. one day i am going
to meet you, and if it is too late, at least i found
out you are not just a name i kept putting into
my words, hoping you would finally see yourself.
one day, my life will be consumed by you, as if it
hadn't been already, but just maybe, i will be able
to tell you about the time i first saw you.

the thing she notices most isn't what you're doing,
it's what you're not saying. women like her see more
than you think and know more than most when it
comes to bravery and pain. she is looking for effort,
quality in your human skills, and your acceptance of
others. she wants to know that you will go out of your
way to help someone else in order to understand if
you will be able to provide the care she needs when
there are no words to be said, as she hides under the
covers and cannot get out of bed. life is about finding
love in the weaknesses prompted by a series of
incalculable disasters. all she is asking from you,
is not to become another storm for her to name.

this morning i awoke as a dreamer,

and as a dreamer goes dreaming,

so does the tide.

even in love,
we must
remain the
wild beasts
we are.
we must
remove all
the human
inside of us
if we are to
ever become
immortal.

as the sun begins to dream,
the moon comes to me with
your naked warmth.

each visit brings promise of
endurance for the lonely
living within me.

my lucid heart whispers,

"there will be a next breath.
there will be a next breath.
there will be a next breath."

between the coffee, rain, flowers, and books,
her life is a kind of story not everyone gets to
be a part of. one where love gathers at the
doorsteps of who you are to welcome in the
new. one where goodbye becomes a single
sentence, instead of an entire chapter.
one where you learn how to fly without
using the wind to keep you above it all.

there is this type of light about her that makes you believe not even all the stars could replicate what she offers. there is this type of vibe about her that makes you believe in miracles, even if one has never greeted you. there is this type of kindness that exudes from her which makes you believe the kid in us all still has a fighting chance to make it out alive. there is this type of strength in her that makes you believe the universe is being held up by her smile alone. there is this broken piece within her, and when the moon hits it just right, you can tell where all the chaos and beauty comes from.

some of us may come from ashes, but our fire
breathes and burns wildly. we are still chasing
anything that makes our soul move. we are
still after anything that makes us smile,
and there are only a few things that can
get us to feel. i can only hope your fire
remains a light for all of those things,
including yourself when the mind goes
dark and the heart goes numb.

even in hell, i found forgiveness
and saw angels never give up
their passion to fly.

        down there, they sing louder
        than the devil's words.

be the spark that ignites
and not destroys.

be the life that comforts
and doesn't surrender.

be the human that stays
instead of running away
in fear of never knowing
what will happen next.

be anything except someone
else and you will see your
life change all at once.

life doesn't get any better than the version i see
with you. you are the precious moment the
universe allowed me to have and i am not
letting go of it. i am here to be close to you
and hold you when love is the only thing
keeping our bones together. you matter,
because you exist. you matter, because i
am not this version of myself without you.
you are the truth dancing on the moon we
look at to know what life is and what it is not.

i love everything i see with you. let me stay in your light. i have grown weary of the darkness and it has grown tired of me. when i speak of you, a new star is born for the world to see. the earth around me will never keep me from protecting you. even when i am crawling to my grave, you will be the reason i won't make it there on time. you've given me hope that even the most tortured of men can find another chance in living again.

there you are,
never promising
me anything
more than what
you can give.
and honestly,
it is the most
attractive quality
about someone
you love.

you be the wind
and i'll be the
arrow.

we will remain above
the chaos and never
fall short.

you are the best kind of love for me. before there was a name attached to who i was, all i ever heard was yours. that's how i know what has happened to me won't ever define me. the only thing i am concerned about, is the smile on your face when you see me. it lets me know i am where i should be, and nothing feels better than knowing you belong to something greater than yourself.

she was covered in wild and found her name in love.
nature nurtured her into becoming someone you
could never forget. out there is where she learned
the language of the flower and the responsibility
of every butterfly.

i don't need a lot of time.

i just need the moments

we make during the time

we have.

you are all that i consumed with.
from body to soul, heart to bones,
you are a creation the gods gave
as a light to follow and a human
to fiercely love. there is you,
then everything else which is
make believe.

i'll whisper in your
ear at 3am and tell
you how much i
love you and how
you aren't what
you think or dream.

loving you, i know how both sides of the moon feel. i know when to hold the sea and kiss the waves. you taught me when looking at someone, to never lose sight of the soul. fluidity lives in you, in what we have, and in what we call beautiful.

this life.

this strength.

this love.

it's always been there.
it's always been yours.

it will wait for until all that is left is my shadow telling you how much the sun loved you. it will wait for you until all that is left is a single star upon a single wave. it will be here, all yours, for however long you need.

she isn't looking for love. she is out here for her chance at freedom. the skies taste like fall and the leaves follow her as she walks throughout the world. her wild was carved from humans who thought they knew her. her eyes speak easy during the night. being vulnerable becomes a trying effort after leaving your skin on the floor of her own bedroom, but even her bones know the truth. wherever she finds herself, it is perfectly made for an extraordinary woman discovering her traveling ways.

my body needs your body.

my soul needs your soul.

my life needs your love.

whenever i look at her, she drops her head a little bit, and it is there, right before her eyes disappear, i fall even harder for this unearthly creature. as soon as she lifts her head once again, i've already proposed a million different times and found another million ways in my head to love her.

i love when you wake up with moon on your hands.

      nothing in this cosmos feels better than
      being woken up to her in my bed,
      bringing me treasures from
      her adventures.

soulmates always find a way
back to where it all began.

as soon as they say hello,
it feels like coming home
again.

all she wanted to do was chase the moonlight and stay as wild as she could until the end.

for her, life was not made to live by rules or suggestions. moon-children live by their own ways.

every once and a while,
when you feel all is lost,
you'll find someone
who means it.

    you'll find someone
    who wants nothing
    more than to stay
    where they said
    they would.

i sat by her, holding her hand, trying to make sense of the day. she was quiet, but i knew stars were colliding in her chest. some days, all you can do is just breathe, and on those days, i will be here, right beside you, breathing in your pain and letting love out.

and on the nights where she
needs you to just lay with
her, you do it. being close
means holding onto the
only thing that matters.

    it means comforting the
    uncomfortable parts
    roaming inside a
    heart that won't
    stay still.

i wonder what will become of us. i wonder how things will turn out. i wonder how many flowers it would take for you to know that love grows everywhere a breath finds you. i wonder how often i could bring you the sun and moon without you feeling the way you do sometimes about your life. there is something beautiful about being kind, and even more so when it is for the one you know you'd like to stay alive forever for, just to never miss them again.

she's not only a woman, but chaos wrapped in flesh.
be careful when approaching her space, because you
will never be able to pick and choose what parts of
her to love. she lives to drink from the waterfalls
of the worlds around her and will never stop
searching for truth that satisfies her taste for
wonderment. it has been a tough life for this
monument of a woman, but she still smiles as
if the wounds don't exist and the tears are a
victory, as they march down her face. we grow
and love without choice, though the reasons behind
them are always evident. we wish to see the imperfect
in everyone we encounter, then are taken by the heart
when we are in the presence of something entirely
made up of pure soil only touched by the wings that
claim they are free. if you think you can love her,
speak and be without an agenda. it is the only way
the fallen can be healed. for some, they don't know
where it hurts and they never quite seem to stop
howling at everything beautiful, because they feel
too much. they tell her to stay calm, but she's the
wildfire others chase after just to feel her burn.

between the sea and stars is where you call home. who you are does not matter. your purpose lives and dies with each unannounced move you make. adventure has created you and mother nature has kept your spirit alive. you will always be every character you've read in your books who have given you power to get through your struggles. you are wolf to some, a lion to others, but a beautiful soul you'll forever be.

you are still my favorite moment
of every sunset we have touched.
where there is light, there is you,
and i know i'll never be without
either.

you are everything that is real to me.
you give me hope and reassurance if
i should ever find myself buried
underneath my own pain, you will
always be able to lift me, like the
moon raises the darkness.

i am grateful for the
randomness that
comes into our lives
and turns into an
unexpected priority
you never thought
could be yours.

i'm not sure if i
will ever have a
grander adventure
than giving you the
stars in my own way.

i hope i can help you see
all the little beautiful
moments of your life.
i hope my eyes are worthy
enough to stay on you
forever.

-i chose to take the long way home-

from your lips to your neck.
from your collarbone to your
breasts. from your fingers to
your stomach. from your hips
to your inner thighs. i remained
patient with your body until we
arrived together where there is
no other feeling like being in
love with a sweet, sweet soul.

there was always a wish she kept for herself. one she knew that would always be hers and no one else's. in her life, she knew humans had the ability to ruin what they have today, for something they never want tomorrow.

what a beautiful life it is to be
sharing the same moon with
you. to not know anything
else about tomorrow except
for love still being a part
of our lives, gives my soul
comfort the same way
stars can heal the sky.

i felt a hand on my shoulder and immediately rolled over to check on her. she looked at me with frustration, and said, "i can't sleep. i've been trying to clear my mind for the last hour." i closed the distance between us, which was only a small space between her breasts and my back. i cradled her and took her into my heart.

"sometimes, beautiful takes longer to sleep, darling. just as the storm outside our window, it will close its eyes once the thunder and lightning both find their rhythm."

she's changed so much in a year and it has
nothing to do with looks. she was born with
beauty misunderstood by everyone. there was
never attention being sought, only respect to
be earned. the way she leans on the universe,
makes you appreciate the summer more in the
way waves only crash for her. there is such an
easy way of breathing about her that makes a
day last a lifetime. a year has created the
woman in her and left the mark of a wolf
on her soul. she's a blood moon who tells
you how it is without hiding her true feelings.
the eyes that sparkle are the same ones you
should be careful with. you never know if they
are planning to escape or hold on with all
they have. if you see her, there's a chance you
will never be able to get her out of your mind.
it's been a year now, and that's all she has
needed to learn what's always been hers to
begin with. her presence makes you believe
in godly things. her smile makes you believe
in getting back up after the fall. her face
reminds you of someone you will never
forget, no matter how many billions of
people may call your name. her love keeps
you safe even if it isn't meant for you.
you can see her wings, but they only come
out for the wild. i wish i had met her sooner,
but time changes us all when we are ready.
this is her life, not mine. i am only an observer
to her light, which when it hits you, feels like
the fresh start you were once promised.

living underneath orion,
time has no color or taste.
it smells of you, and my
life remains perfect.

    it remains something only
    i will ever have with you.

i knew in that moment
if you were to touch me,
i would never stop being
yours. i knew i would
end up kissing you for
the rest of my life.

the way you move your hair from one side to the other for my heart to feel the wind speak. the way your eyes always meet me before you say, "i love you." the way your hands strum the stars when it's too quiet for you. the way you gently move around in bed as you sleep, as if you are trying to find me all over again. i love you without needing anything else but the moments you add to my life. they will be with me each night we have to be apart. the imprint you have pressed onto my soul will never be filled by anyone else. it's where i go when i need to lay with you to feel your comfort before you come back to me.

you are the human
others talk about
spending the rest
of their lives with.

and how goddamn
lucky am i to have
such a thing in
this life of mine.
i know how much
that is, because i
am still nervous
around your beauty.

my favorite smell in the whole universe
is your naked flesh. nothing will ever
take the place of that as long as you are
walking and living next to me. the moon
comes out in you and the sun dies a little
more in me when it does. if you were to
ask me, it is an endearing way to live.
but that's only if you are looking
for an honest fucking answer.

to the nights that make us alive,

may we always run towards each

other with love, love, and

more wild love.

loving you has taught

me how to love all the

things still trying to

find their way.

she laughs like spring
and smells of summer.
a revolution around
the moon and forever
in orbit for the things
she loves. women like
her remain in love with
everything, because they
never forgot what it feels
like to have nothing.

i am yours.

       even in this waiting,

i am yours.

it doesn't matter how old
we grow to be, i will still
adore every inch of your
skin and all of your bones
the same as i did when we
were younger.

    when we were just kids afraid to love
    and only held hands when we were
    scared to leave the other alone.

all i can do is laugh and smile at the
thought of what we could be.

    at what we could become.

        at what we already are.

as long as she is
close to some
earth, she feels
just wild enough
to make anything
her own.

sometimes we meet people and it clicks,
and we go about our lives differently
simply based on encounters. you learn
to see how your eyes can adjust by being
outside of your mind. you learn how love
will never be defined by chasing after what
was never there to begin with. you will learn
how the human body can sleep after losing
something you thought you could never live
without. you will meet these entities, these
otherworldly creatures that give you the reset
you've needed, but could never find. they will
give your lungs resuscitation by removing the
guilt and burden left inside from those who
suffocated the mercy out of you. they will be
the ocean enclosed with flesh and a shelter
made from your broken bones. when they
find you, allow your wounds to speak, your
pain to rest, and your questions to catch fire.
the best hands are the ones who know how
to hold what you never could.

darling,

    not everyone will understand your kind of power. not everyone can make sense of angels, devils, and unearthly things. never hide your truth. never hide your passion. never forfeit your wings. if it's all you have, make sure they know the fight is what keeps you dangerous and unrelenting.

the earth which lives in her voice,
has always been the closest thing
to a home i will ever know. i get
upon my knees as often as i can
to kiss it and savor each word.

your heart has created
the beat in my chest.

now while resting,

      i listen, hold, and love.

you remind me of a star being born;

all chaos. all matter. all precious.

i found my opening
through the openness
you gave to me. i have
never felt more
freedom than being
embraced for who i
am and welcomed for
who i was.

being with you
and making you
laugh for the rest
of your life is the
only thing on my
mind when people
ask me where i
am going.

and then summer brought another opportunity for

    second chances,
    outspoken sunsets,
    and an adventure
    only seen by those
    longing for revival.

trust the wild within the
magic you keep.

the moment you do,
you will never give
up on the things
you love,

including yourself.

home is located in your arms
and where our fingertips
connect earth to air when the
darkness comes for us both.
what we have will never be
made again, and it is for that
reason alone i will never
let you go.

-i will never let your demons say your name-

love will always be
waking up and
catching you in
a dream before
you open your
eyes. it will always
be the opening
breath you take
first before you
look for me.

i kissed you so we wouldn't have to talk. we are just too fucking wild for this world. there are no limits to our fire when all we need is a second alone to be as naked as the rain. i touch you and you feel me. we exist without being casual, because when you know who the other is, you skip the show and tell, and go for the walls and table and anything that can sustain the rigors of obeying your instincts. if at the end of our lives all we have is each other to hold and laugh with, you can lower my body next to yours.

-we carved out our piece of earth long before it took us-

nights that lead to the unforgettable,
become the most meaningful when
you realize how rare of an event
losing yourself with someone you
know nothing about truly is.

    the subtle magic is believing
    in the unknown forces
    behind it all.

the love inside your heart
was placed there by the
moon in your soul.

-you will never be without light-

thank you for loving my life when
i am not always present in it. it takes
that type of love to keep me together.
and sometimes it has been too much
for others. i haven't always been alone,
but it takes sacrifice to be with me,
because i have sacrificed more than
half of mine to find out who i really
was when i had no one else beside me.

life is nothing more than finding your best
friend in someone who loves to take in the
good and bad with you. someone who looks
at you as if you don't know everything,
but still loves you for trying.

you are my heart.
you are my soul.
you are the skin
on my bones.

always close. always near. always with me.

she gets excited about
smelling a sky full of
stars. and these earthly
humans wonder why i
am so fucking crazy
about her.

www.ingramcontent.com/pod-product-compliance
Lightning Source LLC
Chambersburg PA
CBHW021951290426
44108CB00012B/1029